Dedication

To my parents and grandparents
To the Walkups and their farm where my brother and I played as kids

Celebrating the Seasons with Granddad provides a place where children, adults and grandparents can slow down and reconnect with their family history. Written in a simple rhythmic style for young children, the book describes the special relationship between children and their grandparents. Children will enjoy the engaging, quilted illustrations, designed by Judy and her daughter-in-law Kimberly Langley, that are fascinating at every sensory level.

To order additional copies of this book, contact:
Xlibris
844-714-8691
www.Xlibris.com
Orders@Xlibris.com

ISBN: Softcover   978-1-4257-5931-5

Print information available on the last page

Rev. date: 10/25/2023

CELEBRATING the SEASONS with GRANDDAD

Written by **Judy Langley**

Illustrated by **Kimberly Langley & Judy Langley**

My Granddad's farm
is not far away.

We celebrate God's seasons
when I come to stay.

I visit my granddad on hot summer days,
And in fall when the barn's filled
with pumpkins and hay.

I come in the winter when the snowflakes pile high,
And in spring when the wind blows
my kite through the sky.

Summer

In summer time I swing and play,
And stay outdoors each sun drenched day.

I explore the farm just as I please,
And jump and run and climb big trees.

We also saw and hammer and nail,
And camp and fish and hike and sail.

Fall

On crisp autumn days we eat homemade bread
And crunch through the leaves turned all yellow and red.

We gather ripe apples for cobblers and pie,
And watch all the ducks and the geese flying high.

We pick orange pumpkins and jump in the leaves,
And hide in the cornfield behind the dried sheaves.

Winter

January brings the snow
That covers all the earth below.

We dress up warm and romp and run.
Playing in the snow is fun!

Then we sip hot cocoa with marshmallow foam
And munch sugar cookies in Granddad's warm home.

Spring

In spring we tend the garden with care.
We like to work in the sweet smelling air.

We plant corn and tomatoes and carrots and beans,
And melons and cabbage and onions and greens.

We hoe and weed the flower beds
And wear straw hats to shade our heads.

No matter when I come to stay,
We celebrate the seasons day after day.

God's seasons are lovely, as you can see.
God loves His world and Granddad and me.

Fun Family Activities

Country Reading Corner: Display country items: quilts and other handmade toys, rag dolls, dried flower arrangements, pumpkins and gourds, scented candles, canned fruit and veggies, jars of honey, etc. in an area for children. Read books like this one together.

Sorting: Collect buttons and store them in shiny fruitcake tins for kids to sort.

Singing: "My Grandfather's Farm" (Tune: "Old MacDonald")
　　My grandfather has a farm, E-I-E-I-O.
　　And on his farm we planted seeds, E-I-E-I-O,
　　We dig, dig here and we dig, dig there,
　　Here we dig, there we dig, everywhere we dig, dig.
　　My grandfather has a farm, E-I-E-I-O.

Role-Playing: Pretend to fly a kite, plant a garden, cook and bake, camp and fish, build with hammers and nails, dress-up and play in snow.

Activity: Seed Packet Magnet: Buy packets of seeds and "3/4 in." magnetic tape per child. Affix sticky side of tape to back of seed packet. Hot glue a small raffia bow to the front. Give to mothers, grandmothers, or friends.

Activity: Hand Print Flower. Have children dip their hands, palm down, in tempera paint and press hand print petals radiating from a center and forming a circular "flower blossom" on construction/butcher paper. When prints are dry, draw stems and leaves (and possibly a center) with markers or crayons.

Activity: Create a novelty, upside-down photo album of your family. Book one could be photos from the father's family and book two from the mother's. Video relatives and family at home, at work, and at play. It's great fun to show at family reunions and will be cherished by the whole family.

Grandmother's Favorite Recipes

Yummy Sugar Cookies

Sift: 3 C. flour, 1 1/2 t. soda, 1 t. cream of tarter, 1/4 t. salt
Cream: 1/2 C. soft butter, 1/3 C. shortening, 1 1/8 C. sugar,
1/2 t. vanilla, 2 eggs, 1-2 T. milk.
Add: flour to the mixture.

Divide dough into 3 balls. Place in refrigerator 1 hour, until firm.
On a floured surface, roll out dough to 1/4" thickness.
Cut out cookies with cookie cutters.
Bake at 425 degrees on ungreased cookie sheets until done. With a spatula immediately transfer cookies to a flat surface to cool. Decorate with icing and sprinkles and have a tea party!

Campfire Hot Cocoa

Mix: 1/2 C. sugar, 1/3 C. cocoa,
1/4 C. water, 1/8 t. salt
Heat: until sugar melts.
Add: 6 C. milk, 1 t. vanilla.
Heat to taste. Pour cocoa in mugs.
Top with marshmallows!

E-Z Bran Rolls

Mix until dissolved: 3 C. warm water and 2 pkg. yeast.
Mix together: 2/3 C. oil, 1/3 to 3/4 C. sugar, 3 t. salt,
    1 C. bran cereal.
Mix: When bran is soft, stir yeast and bran mixtures together.
Add: 7-8 C. flour (half whole-wheat/half white).
Reserve some flour for kneading. Knead and let rise until double, then punch down.
Oil muffin tins. Grease hands. Squeeze off small balls of dough and place 3 in each muffin cup.
Bake at 350 degrees for 15-20 minutes and then 325 degrees until done. Eat warm with butter and honey!

At Grandmother's house
I have such fun,
Then I'm tucked in with prayer
when the day is done.

Grandmother reads from the Bible to me,
Of Noah's great ark all alone on the sea.

Of young David's harp and Goliath's big fall,
Baby Moses and Joseph and Peter and Paul.

Of Daniel and Esther and Jesus God's Son,
And how God made me special,
His own little one.

A box of photos Grandmother pulls down,
Full of family pictures all faded and brown.

Gram tells about each face we see.
When she was young, she looked just like me!

There are aunts and uncles and cousins and kin,
Gram tells all their stories to me once again.

Gram's sewing room has patterns to pin
And a rainbow of threads and needles so thin.

Gram's button box is shiny and gold,
And I search there for treasure like pirates of old.

I sift my loot as I explore,
And I sort all the buttons on Grandmother's floor.

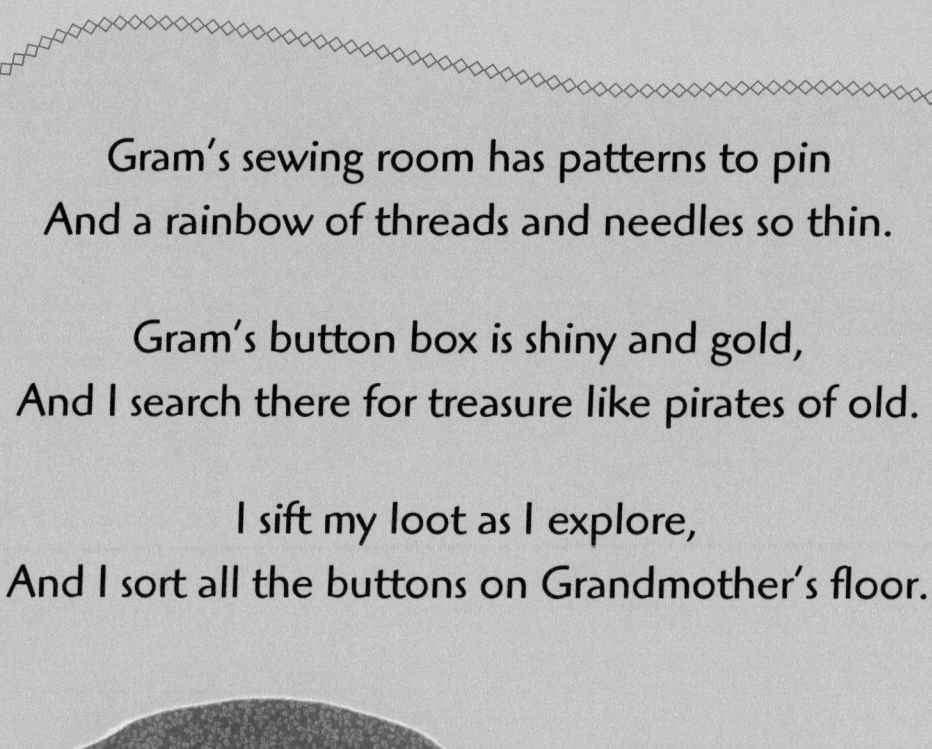

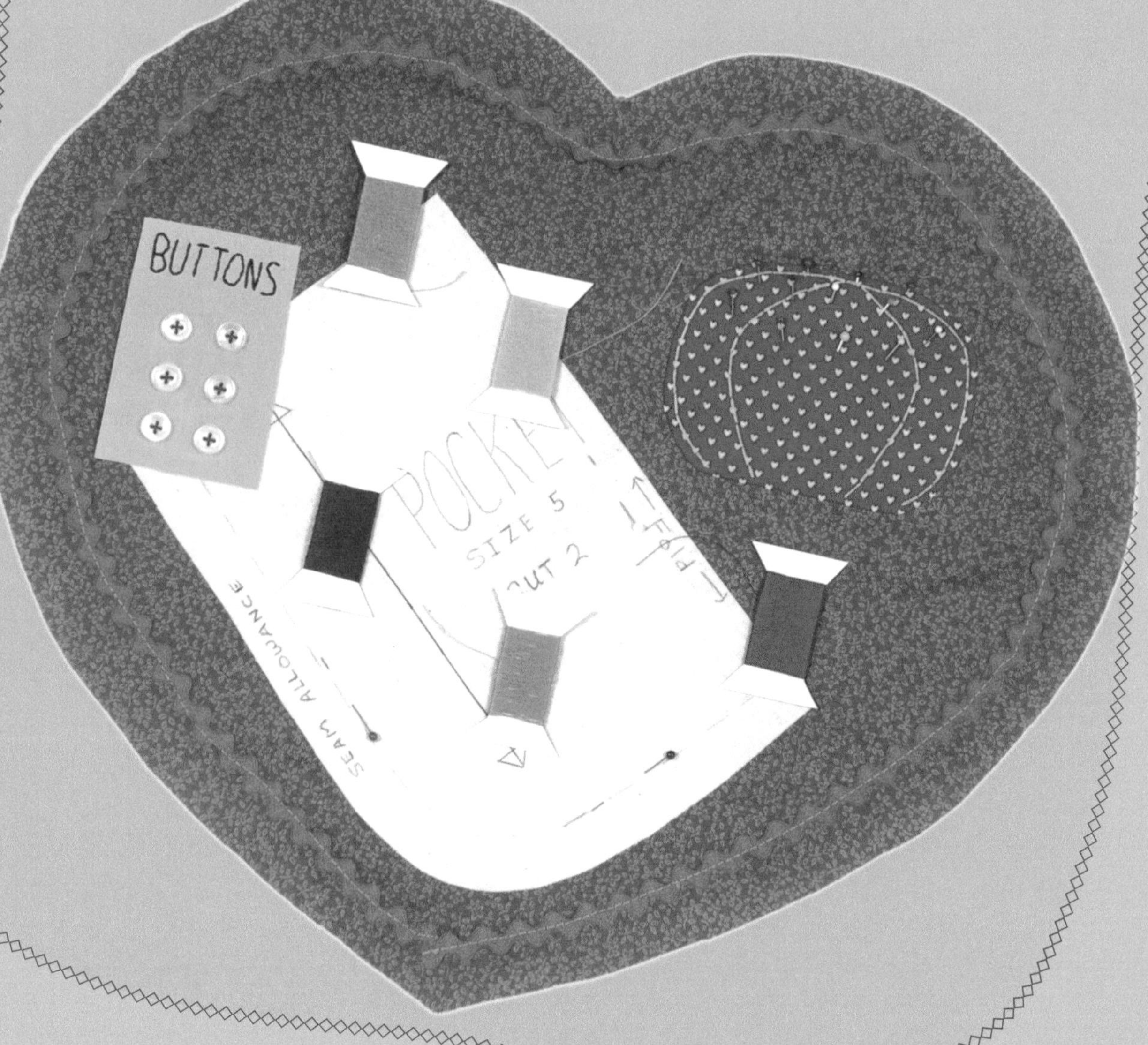

Grandmother's kitchen is cozy and nice
And smells like a bakery
with sugar and spice.

I like to help Grandmother mix up each treat.
We make cookies and candy
and sweet things to eat.

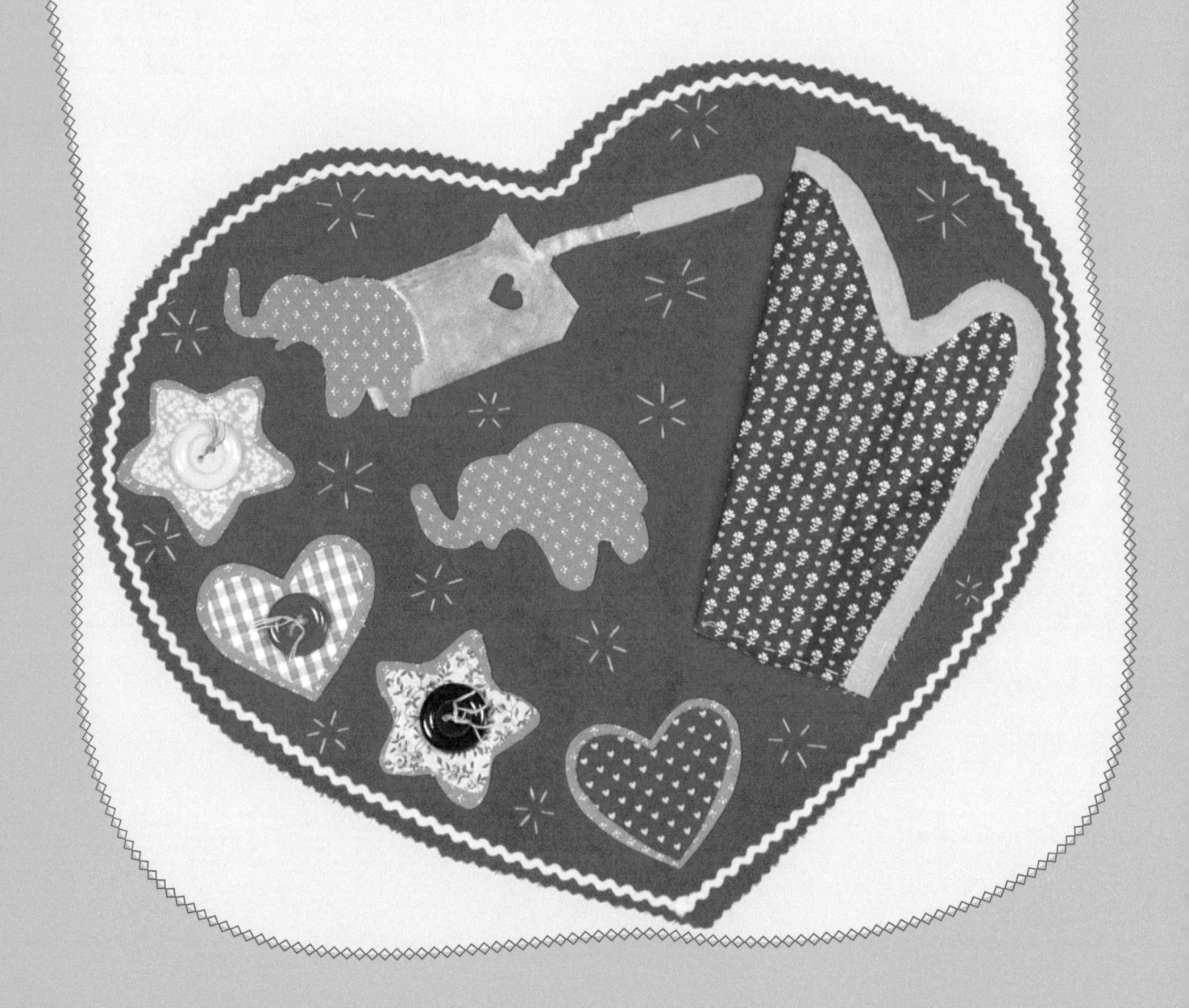

The big red barn is full of sounds,
Moos and grunts and neighs abound.

There are hogs to slop and cows to milk,
And we pet all the kittens that feel soft as silk.

We gather eggs, and feed hungry chicks,
Then Gram cooks up pancakes with syrup poured thick.

My Grandmother's house is not far away.
We have fun together when I come to stay!

Gram makes me feel special and listens with care
To all of the stories that I like to share.

COZY DAYS
WITH GRANDMOTHER

Written by **Judy Langley**

Illustrated by **Kimberly Langley & Judy Langley**

Dedication

To My Far-Flung Family

Son-Anthony and Kimberly Langley

Christa Nicoal and Cora Camille born in England

Thane Edward—Germany and Lance Anthony—Colorado

Son-Jonathan and Laura Langley

Keely Christiona—Ireland and Jadon Philip—England

Judy Langley graduated from Wayland Baptist University and married her high school sweetheart, Phil Langley. Judy and Phil taught school in New Mexico and Oregon before serving as missionaries in Zimbabwe and Togo. They have also worked with churches in Colorado, New Mexico, Hawaii and California. In California Judy published 6 mission adventure books for preschoolers and children with New Hope Publishers. She directed California Christian Writers' Fellowship and served as Stateside Prayer Coordinator for the Celtic Languages Team. Since moving back to Colorado, Judy spends most of her time traveling with Phil, entertaining, and working with churches in the Continental Divide Association of Southern Baptist Churches where she serves as ministry assistant. Judy enjoys hiking, picnicking and 4-wheeling in the Rocky Mountains; reading, writing, speaking for women's groups and singing in a quartet with friends; and creating special books for her grandchildren. Judy has 2 sons, 2 daughters-in-law and 6 grandchildren who continually inspire her to write.

To order additional copies of this book, contact:
Xlibris
844-714-8691
www.Xlibris.com
Orders@Xlibris.com

ISBN: Softcover   978-1-4257-5931-5

Print information available on the last page

Rev. date: 10/25/2023

Printed in the United States
by Baker & Taylor Publisher Services